TALKIN' BASEBALL

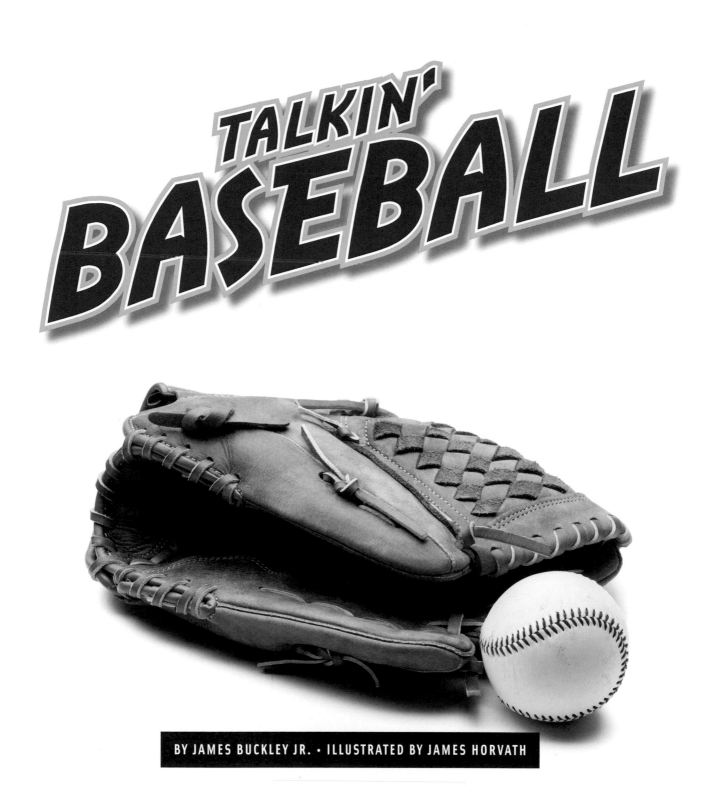

BY JAMES BUCKLEY JR. · ILLUSTRATED BY JAMES HORVATH

The Child's World®

Published by The Child's World®
1980 Lookout Drive • Mankato, MN 56003-1705
800-599-READ • www.childsworld.com

Photographs
Cover: Eugene Onischenko/Shutterstock
Interior: Newscom: Jim Ruymen/UPI 5, 10400 8
inset, Bill Greenblatt/UPI 16, John Korduner/Icon
19; Joe Robbins: 4, 6, 7, 8, 9, 10, 11, 14, 17; Shutter-
stock: Mtsaride 1, Sirtravelot 13T, Aspen Photo 18.

ISBN 9781503835719
LCCN 2019943129

Printed in the United States of America

TABLE OF CONTENTS

INTRODUCTION

Baseball's nickname? America's National Pastime

"The hot corner really flashed the leather when he scooped up that scorcher!" If you don't "talk" baseball, that sentence made no sense. This book is here to help! Every sport has its own language. Each sport's words and phrases mean something to true fans. The more of those words you can learn, the more you'll enjoy every game you watch. In this book, we'll explore baseball. Batter up!

Mookie Betts shows how a batter finishes swinging the bat. ▶

Famous Nicknames

"Old Hoss" Radbourn

Babe "The Sultan of Swat" Ruth

Lou "The Iron Horse" Gehrig

"Shoeless" Joe Jackson

World or World's?

The championship of Major League Baseball (MLB) is the World Series. The winners of the American and National Leagues meet to see who is number one. The first World Series was in 1903. It was called the World's Series. The current name began to stick in the 1910s.

▲ The MLB champ gets the Commissioner's Trophy. It is named for the job title of the person who runs MLB.

Hi! I'm here to tell you more cool baseball words!

One Word or Two?

People started playing a baseball-like game in the 1840s. At first, they called it "base ball." It was not until after the **Civil War** (1861–1865) that the name turned into a single word.

Tops are called jerseys. Baseball pants used to be knickers. Players wear caps on their heads—never hats! Baseball gear has not changed a lot from the sport's early days. Here are some ways to talk about what players use and wear.

▲ *Some players wear their long pants pulled up. That makes the pants look like old-time knickers.*

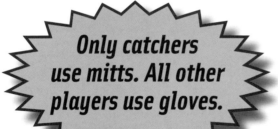

Only catchers use mitts. All other players use gloves.

The Ball

One nickname for a baseball is the "old horsehide." That's because early balls were made from horse leather. The stitches on a baseball are called seams. Some pitches have "seam" in their name, such as the "four-seam fastball."

The Glove

Great **defensive** players "flash the leather." That means they're the best at using their leather gloves. Many players also wear thin leather gloves when they are batting.

▲ Catchers wear gear to protect them from balls, bats, and collisions.

Catcher's Gear

Catchers need the most protection. They wear plastic shin guards and a heavy chest protector made of cloth and leather. A catcher's mask is made of metal and plastic. The helmets they use are thick plastic.

The Bat

Players in the Major Leagues use bats made of wood, such as ash, hickory, or maple. High schools and some youth leagues use aluminum bats. Some people call a bunch of bats "the lumber."

ON THE FIELD

A nickname for the catcher? Call him the backstop.

▲ *A batter swings at a pitch that is over home plate. If he misses, the catcher catches it!*

The Diamond

A baseball field is called a diamond. Each side is 90 feet (27.4 m) long. That's the distance between each base. The fourth base is not called a base. It's called home plate. It is a pentagon, with five sides.

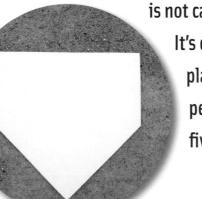

The Foul Poles

A tall metal pole stands at each corner of the outfield. If a ball hits the pole, it is a fair ball. White lines on the field show the fair and foul areas.

▼ In and Out

The diamond and the dirt around it are the infield. The large grass area behind the infield is the outfield. Three fielders cover this huge space. Padded fences stand at the back of the outfield. If a ball flies over the fence, it's a home run.

◄ The Mound

The bump in the middle of the diamond is the pitcher's mound. The mound is raised about 10 inches (25.4 cm) above the grass. The pitcher stands on the mound with one foot on a large chunk of rubber. The rubber is 60 feet, 6 inches (18.44 m) from home plate.

◄ The Dugout

Baseball players sit down a lot! When their team is batting, they watch their teammates and wait for their turn to bat. They do that from the dugout. In most ballparks, this area is below the level of the field. It looks like it was "dug out" like a trench.

PLAYING THE GAME

It's time to use your lumber to hit some cheese thrown over the dish!

Did you get all that?

The *lumber* is the wood bat. *Cheese* is a nickname for a fastball. And the *dish* is home plate! Let's take a tour through words you hear during baseball action.

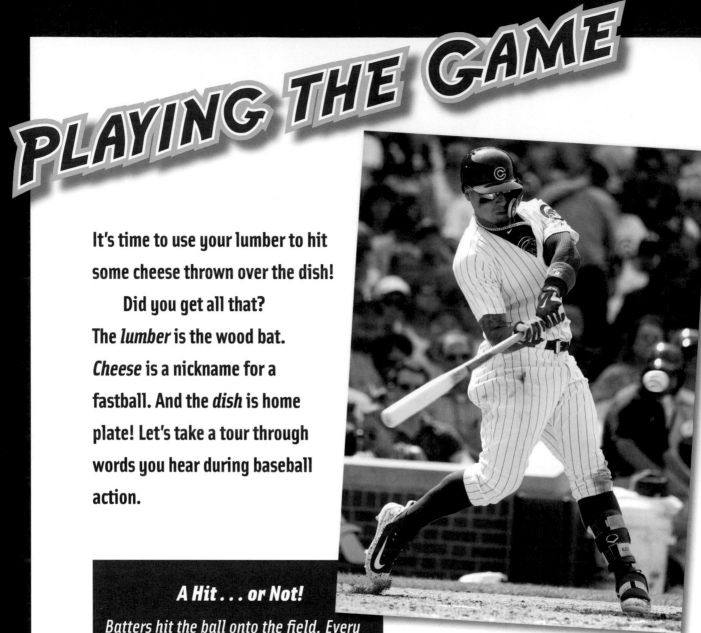

▲ *A batter takes a hack! That means he is swinging hard at the pitch.*

A Hit . . . or Not!

Batters hit the ball onto the field. Every time they hit it, it's not a hit! It's only called a hit if they reach base safely and the defense doesn't mak an error. Otherwise, they are out. After three outs, the teams switch places.

Pitching

"A rubber-armed hurler fired some chin music after he came in as the closer."

A pitcher who can throw a lot of innings was throwing the ball very near the batters. This pitcher was in to finish, or "close out," the game. Pitchers can be starters, **relievers**, or closers.

▲ *Pitchers have many nicknames, such as hurler, fireballer, and moundsman.*

Hitters reach base with singles, doubles, and triples.

Hitting

"The slugger ripped a frozen rope into the gap and pulled up with a two-bagger."

A powerful hitter smashed a **line drive** between two outfielders. He ran all the way to second base.

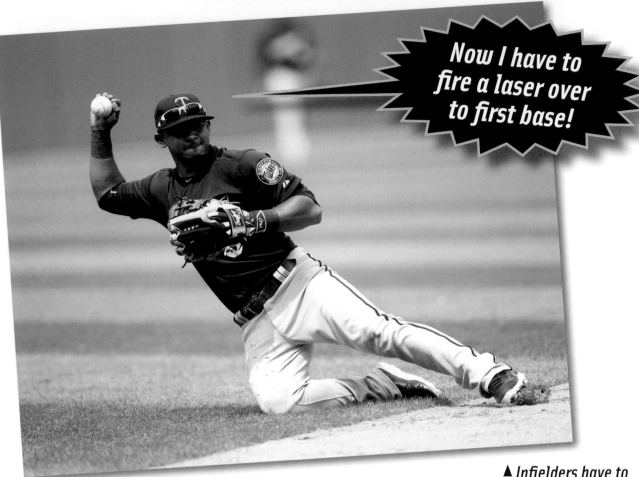

Now I have to fire a laser over to first base!

▲ Infielders have to move quickly to scoop up ground balls (called "grounders").

Fielding

"The slick-fielding shortstop went into the hole to barehand a worm burner and then threw a pea to first."

The fielder between second and third moved to his right (the "hole" between him and the third baseman). He used his hand, not his glove, to pick up a ball skimming along the grass. Then he threw very hard to first base.

Baserunning

"The speedster burst from his lead and churned dirt before belly flopping in ahead of the tag. Stolen base!"

A very fast runner ran from first to second base. He dove headfirst and touched the base before the fielder touched him with the ball. Getting to a base this way meant the runner "stole" the base.

▼ *The player in red here is about to steal second base. He'll touch the base before the fielder can tag him with the ball.*

STAT CITY

I think that one is "going yard"!

Baseball is a game with lots of numbers. Knowing about these important statistics can teach you a lot about baseball.

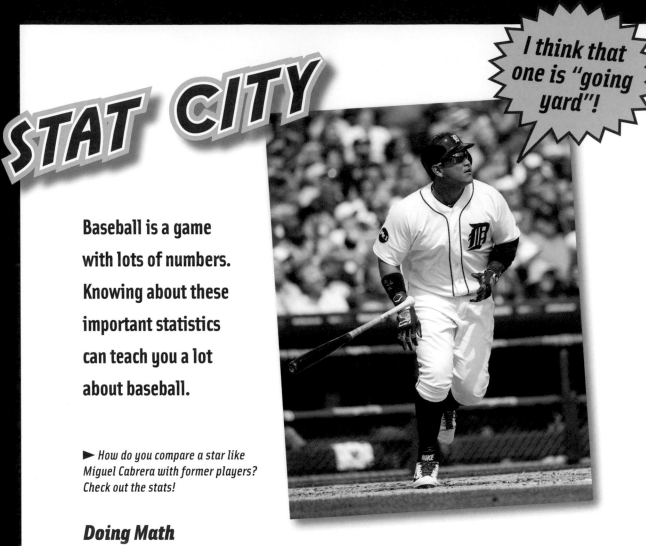

► How do you compare a star like Miguel Cabrera with former players? Check out the stats!

Doing Math

Batting Average (BA): Divide the number of hits by the number of **at bats**. A good batting average is above .300.

Slugging Average (SA): Divide the number of total bases by the number of at bats. A good slugging average is .450 or higher.

Earned Run Average (ERA): Multiply a pitcher's earned runs by 9. Then divide that number by the number of innings pitched. Great pitchers have ERAs under 3.00.

OPS and WHIP

OPS is a player's **O**n-base percentage **P**lus **S**lugging average. Many experts think this is a better measurement than a player's batting average. OPS measures how often a player gets on base. It also looks at how many big hits the player gets. The higher the OPS number, the better.

WHIP stands for **W**alks plus **H**its for each **I**nning **P**itched. This measures (mostly) how many baserunners a pitcher allows.

Keeping Track

Hitters keep track of hits, runs, singles, doubles, triples, and home runs. Pitchers count strikeouts, wins, walks, and innings pitched. Fielders tally up chances (each time they try to catch the ball). They hope to avoid too many **errors**.

Cuadrangular is Spanish for home run!

Homers

The biggest hit in baseball is the home run—when a player runs all of the bases. Most of the time, the batter knocks the ball out of the ballpark. Here are some great nicknames for homers.

- Going yard
- Dinger
- Big fly
- Touch 'em all
- Tater
- Longball

15

BASEBALL PEOPLE

Players, coaches, umpires, and fans all pack into the ballpark for every game. Some of them have some fun nicknames.

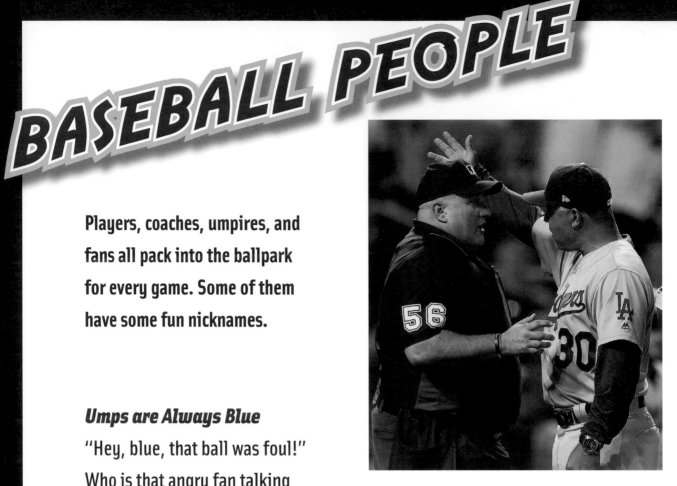

▲ *Managers sometimes disagree with umpires. They have a pleasant chat (but sometimes they yell!).*

Umps are Always Blue

"Hey, blue, that ball was foul!" Who is that angry fan talking to? The umpire! Umpires make all the calls in a game. They say who is safe or out. They call balls and strikes at home plate. A nickname for any umpire comes from their old uniforms, so you can call them "Blue."

Who's the Skipper?

The person in charge of the team on the field is the manager. He sets the lineup of positions and batting order. He decides when to replace the pitcher. Even if you don't know the manager's name, he'll always answer to "Skip" or "Skipper."

At the hot corner, I have to be ready for anything!

◄ *All fielders move into this "ready position" as the pitch is thrown to home plate.*

The "DH"

For years, people watched pitchers try to hit...badly. Nearly all pitchers were terrible at hitting! In 1973, baseball added a new position. The designated hitter (DH) replaces the pitcher in the batting lineup. Every league in the world uses the DH now except the National League!

At Third

One of the best nicknames for a baseball position is for third base. These fielders are usually closest to the batters. They have to grab hard-hit ground balls and super-fast line drives. For these reasons, third base is known as "the hot corner."

FUN STUFF

Baseball has been around for a long time. Fans and players have come up with some great nicknames, words, and terms to describe the game!

▲ Why "can of corn"? The term comes from when store clerks caught cans knocked off high shelves!

Banjo hitter

This is a hitter who doesn't have a lot of power.

Can of corn

This is a fly ball that is easy to catch.

Comebacker

Pitchers need to watch for these hits. They come right back to the pitcher!

On Their Backs

Every player has a number on the back of his jersey. Using jersey numbers began in 1929. The first numbers were given to players based on the batting order. So the great Babe Ruth wore #3 because he batted third. Teams can also "retire" a number. A truly great player will be honored that way. When a player's number is retired, no player can ever wear that number again for that team.

Foot in the bucket

This describes a batter who steps away from the plate when he swings.

Frozen rope

This is a hard line drive that looks like a frozen rope as it zings through the air.

Hitters have batting practice before games. Call it "B.P."

Golden sombrero

If a hitter strikes out four times in a game, he earns this silly nickname.

Noodle arm

A player who can't throw the ball very hard has a noodle arm.

Rally cap

When your team is behind, flip your cap around or upside down to bring good luck!

◄ *What does your team do for rally caps? This version is called The Shark.*

LATEST SLANG

Baseball has been around for more than 175 years. Some of the words from long ago are rarely heard today. However, modern players and fans are still coming up with new fun ways to talk about their game.

Dialed in
Being dialed in means really seeing and hitting the ball well.

Knee buckler
This is a curveball that fools a batter.

The rock
The rock is the baseball!

◄ *A knuckleball is a type of pitch. It moves in odd ways. And pitchers use their fingertips to throw a knuckleball . . . not their knuckles.*

Sabermetrics

Sabermetrics is the nickname for all the fancy new stats that baseball uses.

Snow cone

This is a catch in which the ball sticks out of the top of the glove.

Web gem

This is a great fielding play that will be on the internet for sure!

Yakker

A yakker is a curveball.

▼ *After a long run, this outfielder snagged the ball with a snow cone catch.*

GLOSSARY

aluminum (uh-LOO-min-um) a very lightweight metal

at bat (AT BAT) term for when a player stands at home plate

Civil War (SIV-ul WAR) conflict between Northern and Southern United States from 1861 to 1865

defensive (dee-FEN-siv) describing the team in the field

designated (DEZ-ig-nay-ted) specially chosen for a job

errors (AYR-urz) mistakes

knickers (NIK-urz) old-fashioned types of pants that ended just below the knees

line drive (LINE DRYV) a hit in baseball that goes very straight

relievers (ruh-LEE-vurz) pitchers who come into a game after the starting pitcher leaves

sultan (SUL-tan) a royal title

Thanks for reading! See you at the ballpark.

FIND OUT MORE

IN THE LIBRARY

Johnson, Varian. *What Were the Negro Leagues?*
New York, NY: Penguin Workshop, 2019.

Kelley, David. *The Ballpark Mysteries: Starting Lineup.*
New York, NY: Random House Books for Young Readers, 2019.

Sports Illustrated Editors. *Baseball: The Big Book of Who.*
New York, NY: Sports Illustrated Kids, 2017.

ON THE WEB

Visit our Web site for links about baseball:

childsworld.com/links

*Note to Parents, Teachers, and Librarians: We routinely verify our Web links to make sure
they are safe and active sites. So encourage your readers to check them out!*

INDEX

About the Author and Illustrator

James Buckley Jr. is the author of more than 100 books on sports for young readers, as well as many sports biographies. He lives in Santa Barbara, California. James Horvath is an illustrator and cartoonist based in California. He has written and illustrated several children's books, including Dig, Dogs, Dig! and Build, Dogs, Build!